"Reuben Jackson's *My S*  ching
parting gift from one of idian
in each of these intimate ....c takes its reader
on a roadtrip through the lens of a nerdy Black dude from D.C. but
stationed in Vermont. These poems reveal the poet in solidarity with
nature, yet self conscious and hyper aware of his otherness. These
poems may well be the answer to the question many of us struggle
with: How can we as humans feel less alone?"

—Abdul Ali, author of *Trouble Sleeping*

"Reuben Jackson's poems are beautiful, crystalline structures
demonstrating that he was more of a Vermonter than most of us will
ever be even if he was actually from Washington D.C. Although he
was deeply attached to this place [Vermont] and these mountains,
Reuben's spirit is truly universal—his words speak to everyone who
cares about language, music, and engagement with the world. He
will be deeply missed in his embodied form but with these poems his
voice will remain resonant and very deeply alive."

—Christopher Kaufman Ilstrup, executive director of
Vermont Humanities

"The inimitable spirit of Reuben Jackson is wholly in these poems, so-
phisticate connoisseur of all things humane and beautiful: friends,
family, music, 'October light' as 'an answered prayer.' Wide-eyed and
ever aware of the pitch of history, Jackson's mind is the gathering we
need now and tomorrow."

—Major Jackson, poet, professor, and author of
six books of poetry, including *Razzle Dazzle*

My Specific Awe and Wonder

My Specific Awe and Wonder

poems and what not

by Reuben Jackson

Rootstock Publishing

Montpelier, VT

Published by Rootstock Publishing
an imprint of Ziggy Media LLC
Montpelier, Vermont 05602
info@rootstockpublishing.com
www.rootstockpublishing.com

Softcover ISBN: 978-1-57869-178-4
Library of Congress Number: 2024941268

Cover photo and author photo by Reuben Jackson.
Book design by Eddie Vincent, ENC Graphic Services.

Contents

For Reuben

a tribute poem by Rajnii Eddins, author of Their Names Are Mine

Reuben
Did a flock of doves
Spirit away on notes of Sonny Rollins
The day you flew home
Did Kelly take a trip to the barbershop
And feel a blue melody
Aching furiously and fiercely
One that made him smile
Tenderly
at the 5-year-old getting his haircut
For the first time
in the chair across from him
Did whispers of memories
only held by chosen
rememberers
Have occasion to rise
on scattered clouds
cross the winds that day
Saying
"This is Honey"
Reuben, are you somewhere
I know you're somewhere
Trailing light across the heavens
Walking
in that life-sized heart of yours
Your words
tinged with tender
wit and candor
And so much *us*
Yes, you are somewhere
Bravely breaking tropes
In your vivid
unapologetic shy and awkward grace

Reuben
I miss my friend
I miss the talks we never had
But it's something like
what I told
A friend recently
Something bout
How
To lose someone
To lose
anything
You had to have had it
Once
You had to have them
first
And this world
don't even know
How lucky it was
Is
We got to have you

Dear Reader,

Reuben Jackson's voice first flowed into my life like wildflower honey on a hot summer's day. It was warm, and rich, and sweet. Listening was an indulgence. His words married his love of music, understanding of history, and hope for humanity. Music he shared transported me back to when I was a nappy-headed child. Standing on the coffee table. Wearing cotton pj's. Singing off-key with Billie Holiday into my hairbrush. Album covers were proudly displayed alongside family photos and the Encyclopedia Britannica. Many of those albums were featured on *Friday Night Jazz*. Thelonious, Ella, and Charlie were all there. On the radio, Reuben Jackson was a time machine.

In-person, for me, Reuben became intricate origami. There was no face attached to his voice. When I encountered another melanin rich human in Vermont, I gave a nod of recognition. This was the first fold. With repeat encounters, Nods grew into smiles. Fold. I noted he laughed a lot. Fold. He was always greeted warmly by others. Fold. He responded in kind. Fold. Nods and smiles evolved into waves. Fold. I shared my poetry at a gathering. He was in attendance. Afterwards, he came to me and in that voice said, "Thank you." Fold. He took the mic. I heard his poetry for the first time. Fold. Fold. Fold. All of those folds came together until we held respect and friendship between us. Face-to-face, Reuben Jackson was a friend.

Reading *My Specific Awe and Wonder* is like standing outside a large display window in shifting sunlight. One moment the world of Reuben's poetry is illuminated on the other side of the pane separate from you. Then a shadow drifts and suddenly you're staring at your own reflection. When the light is just right and the words of the poems settle somewhere within, your image becomes part of the world of Reuben's words. On the page, Reuben Jackson is embracing.

—LN Bethea, Vermont poet and activist

I. Good Fences

"Good fences make good neighbors."
–Robert Frost

Two City Boys

Two city boys
Spent an autumn Sunday
Hugging the right lane
Of Interstate
14.

We marveled
At the way
Robert Frost's Mending Wall
Rolled across the hills like music—

Followed us to Canada like
A runaway slave

Through Hardwick, Craftsbury, East Craftsbury,
Craftsbury Common, Mill Village,
West Glover,

As foliage rattled like pom-poms cheering us on.

Country Music

White men guard the six foot space
Separating my table from the nearest blonde.

I am as nervous as a guitarist
Moments from an audition with Merle Haggard.

When a fight destroys the picture window
Should I join in on the laughter?
Would my silence be perceived as uppity?

A man the size of Texas buys me a beer,
Then asks if the lead singer would make it in the soul field.
He wants an answer.

An hour later
He's stuffing the jukebox
As if it is a collection plate at the church of Ferlin Husky.

He plays nothing but love songs—
Just like my Dad.

East Barre

The salesclerk claimed that the snow fell
With a Vermont accent.

I only knew that the cords I bought from L.L. Bean
Had not been purchased in vain,

And that here, no one seemed to fight
For the last roll of toilet paper from
An otherwise empty grocery store shelf.

The latter miracle was reason enough to call my Southern kin,
Whose minds were also filled with Central Casting notions
Of the world of above Boston.

But the weather owned my eyes
Like the gazebo at the foot of Main Street—
Where I quietly wept while waiting for Jimmy Stewart's
Ghost.

Two Vermont Vignettes

1. East Montpelier

A tall, beardless man
Sidles up.
I am
To his knowledge
The first colored person
Ever to attend the annual
Thanksgiving Venison extravaganza.
Welcome, he says.
I can't speak for the others—
But I am sure the venison
Doesn't mind.

2. Facing the Adirondacks

I stand before the
Frozen lake.
My breath a series
Of short lived
Clouds.
Lord please
Let me die here.

Sunday Afternoon
East Glover, Vermont

Two lane roads
Twist like an awkward boy
At a house party

Chamber of Commerce
Autumnal breezes say
"It's ok to be
A middle aged
October smitten brother
In a corny plaid jacket
Which screams
I too fell in love
With Technicolor fairy tales
About this place!"

I am a concrete weary man
En route to a tryst with trees
And silence.

I wave to blushing hills—
Check the rear-view mirror
For police
Suffering from a draught of quotas.

But now it is as calm
As a day in which
My blackness is unsettling
To the woman in the
General Store.

Autumns

My big brother's jump shot
Is as flawless as the crease
In God's khakis.

I quietly swoon
Between bites of my Mother's tuna on rye,
And the things I whisper
To the growing shadows.

The October light
Is an answered prayer.

1975

Walking by the
Winooski River
Between classes.
Omnipresent
Salmon-colored dusk.

The wind says
"Reuben—I'm afraid you're a romantic."
"Don't snitch"
I reply.

An old beagle
Stops to sniff the hem
Of my bell bottoms.

A tear makes its way to my
Third eye.

To the White Man Staring in the General Store
Enosburg Falls, Vermont, September 2015

We have been here
Since the first
Astonished slave ships
Did their
Blue business.

A lynched foundation.
The unacknowledged source
Of Old Glory's Red.

Even the Elvis
You listen to at home
Is dipped in blackness.

As are the rapidly rapped lines
Your granddaughter
Recites in the
Dark.

Watching Soul Train with Thomas
St. Johnsbury, Vermont, May 1975

How do your people shake
Like windblown leaves?

And why have I never seen you
as loose as a beagle?

He laughed until
Tears rolled like
Maple sap
Into buckets
When winter
Shimmies ice
Off of the rivers

And spring makes its way
To the club.

Black in Vermont #9
Summer 2017 Mix

You're a nigger.

A public radio
Treasure.
A public radio
Nigger Treasure.

10:00 A.M.
A neighbor smiles
In the elevator.

10:05.
I'm followed to the
Radio station
By the Cops.

I Asked a Certain Maple

For its phone number.
Not for me
I insisted
But for my
Bedroom window
So when the
October wind
Comes to visit
The sound of
Soon to be vanished
Leaves
Knocking against
The glass
Like inspiration
(Or a lover's head
Meeting the headboard)
Will conspire
To briefly evict
The posse
Of sorrows
From my brain
Like a bartender
Serving
A 90 Proof Glass
On the house.

Long Distance Love

A friend sends
A picture of three chickens
Standing in a kind of
Formation
On a road where
The snow has begun
To retreat.

Funny
I tell her
I was humming the theme from
Green Acres last evening
And thinking about people
Who move to rural places
In search of serenity
While also yearning
For a Trader Joe's.

As for myself
I remain smitten with
Mountains
Majestic but
Unpretentious

And the way
Rural silence calms me
Like Miles Davis playing
A ballad.

A serenity
My friend says he finds
In the
Ever changing
Sky.

Dear Montpelier

You are in me
Like Coltrane's sound.

Some things just are.

They need no mini series
Or Facebook post.

Your streets are home.

Home is not an Exclamation
Or polysyllabic treatise.

Some things just are.

II. *Kelly Donaldson*

I was introduced to the reclusive extrovert known as Kelly Donaldson by a mutual friend back in 1973. Our friend knew we shared a deep love for what old heads like us call "the word," even if we were reluctant to run around the city telling people about it.

Kelly and I also share a love for Turner Classic Movies, independently owned coffee shops, bean pies, autumn, and the music of Claude Debussy.

After six months or so, he shared some of his ruminations. I immediately fell in love with his candor, honesty, and his bittersweet lyricism. When I asked why he had not attempted to publish them, he said nothing.

Later that same day, he said that if I ever managed to get a book deal, he'd send me a few to include in said volume, provided I credited him. I also agreed to split any royalties.

The following poems are, in Kelly's words, "a few of my better attempts at making sense of our 20 minutes on this planet."

We both hope you like them.

Kelly on Middle Age

I like glaring at
Phone addicted young'uns
Who hog the seats
Set aside for seniors
Until they take their
Blank gazes elsewhere

I also love talking
Old school music
With the coffee shop crew

We have no money
(Fixed incomes, yo!)
No girlfriends
And no more verbal reticence

Some days
My boy Melvin said recently
"My knees creak like coffin handles in need of
3 in 1 oil!"

There used to be more of us
Laughing at his jokes.

Kelly Recalls 1963

I still call
The year 1963
Season of Nightmares

After Medgar Evers was killed
I would lie awake and wait for
Uncle joe to get home safely

He and Aunt Blanche
Had the same kind of carport
Mr. Evers had

I know because I read
An article about his assassination
Over and over
In *Ebony* magazine

Even when my Uncle
Was safely sleeping
On the couch
I could not rest
Because I now knew
That we were hated
For being who we were
And are

Then the four little girls in Birmingham
Died in that bombing

Who will protect us I
Asked the moon
On countless Southern
nights.

Kelly Makes It Plain

People ask why
A lot of
My stuff
Has three words
On each line
It's cause I
Do what I
Want with my
How you say
Ruminations but really
It's because waltzes
Are in ¾
Time and I
Am paying that
Much loved form
Some respect alright?

Kelly Donaldson's Blues in ¾ Time

I longed to waltz with Brenda
But it was 1968
And Johann Strauss
Was not on
The Hit Parade

And even if he was
She would have said
Take your nerdy ass home and read
A book about Strauss
Or some other counter-revolutionary
Nonsense

I was in love with her
So I saved her
The trouble of raising her
Beautiful voice
And walked out.

Kelly on Francine

I talk a lot
Say a million things
Some have never seen
The light of day

We chat for hours
(Only once did my tongue
Ask for a breather)

I don't hate many things
But one of them is
Saying goodbye

Kelly Writes:

I keep my head
On swivel

So I (hopefully)
Don't become

Black history

In this
Or any other

Month.

III. Travels

Danish Sketches

I. Arrival in Denmark

What's it like?
My Mother asked.

When I hail a cab
They stop!—
(My words excitedly
Panted across the water.)

That's all you have to say?
She retorted.

What else is there—
I sighed.

II.

Look out for
Pickpockets
The kind concierge
Said
To a man
From a city
Which ended
The previous year
With 300
Homicides.

III.

What's a hyper curious
Black boy
From the intersection of
Motherfucker and
Debussy
Doing on a
Relaxed park
Bench on
A beautiful day
In Tivoli Gardens?

And why are all
These white people
Smiling
In my direction?
It's some kind of hustle—
Right?

IV. At Ben Webster's Grave

Every morning
I walk the tree lined path
To his stone

My question
An awkward song refrain:

Were you happier here?

The cabbie who
Drove me from the
Airport
Called you a hero
The moment I mentioned
Your name.

Key West
October 1963

You could have
Buried Emmett Till
Beneath that
Pound of sugar
At the bottom
Of the Dixie cup
I was handed
(minus lemon)
Through the Jim Crow
Window of
Peaches' Café

I swore I saw a blonde
Smile at me
Through the
Fancy restaurant
Window

But Mother said she
Was picking stone crab
From between her teeth

And to turn my eyes
Toward heaven

Where it seemed
Even the sky and clouds
Sat apart.

63rd and Broadway

My hotel room is small.
No space for leaves
That haunt the idle fountains
Of Lincoln Center.

Who's the statue
In the nearby park?
(Its benches lined with
Shadows.)

Down the street
Is the church where Billie Holiday's funeral was held—
And to the West—
The lower-case skyline of New Jersey.

Gazing across the Hudson,
I don't think of Bruce Springsteen,

But of Thelonious Monk
Resisting the piano's advances,
And the city where I am happiest alone.

Tee
Washington, DC

A Bic lighter
Cranked to the max

The tear-shaped flame
Sparks a pipe
Whose smoke surges
Like young brothers
Entering a theater

To watch John Wayne
Eliminate entire tribes
With a single bullet

Before the box of Raisinets™
Is opened like your eyes
When the pusher comes

7th Grade

My anxious life
Catches its breath

On a path
Beneath
A crosstown
Posse of maples

Who have no
Interest
In snatching the bus fare
In my pocket

I swear I heard the August breeze
Whisper

Are you sure you want to
Go back home?

Neighbors, 1990

They turned everything up to 10:
Arguments, bath water,
Gospel music.

Did I mention Commodores albums?
Do you want to know what hell is?

Being bedridden with the Flu,
And hearing Lionel Richie singing
"Easy Like Sunday Morning"
Twenty or thirty times.

Old Music

Writing poems
About old music
Is beginning to make me feel like
One of those relatives
You consciously avoid
At gatherings

The ones who think
Today's music is alright

But just let them tell you about some ghost
They saw at the Fillmore, The Apollo Theater—
Wherever

I don't think a lifelong passion for Hendrix
Puts me in that boat

But this isn't the same as discovering
One's blackness in the mirror, baby

It's more like a chive on your tooth
Spaghetti stains on your sweater

Everyone's giggling
You're the last to know

It's Hard to Believe

I'm still the geeky dude sweating
In the bleachers
At the Friday night
Middle school
Dance.

The Call
11th Grade

Never once had I seen a poet
In dull brown orthopedic shoes
Thick, nerdy glasses?
Yes.

The stoop I nursed was my
Mending Wall—
A semi-respite from the neighborhood's rage.

Who knew that beneath my guarded gaze,
I was rifling through my head
For words I'd use to praise mountains?

Promises, Promises

The next woman
Who calls me Reub
Might be asked
To chip in on a bottle
Of anti-swoon medication.

Or she might receive a poem
Written after I asked the evening sky
For a phrase rhyming with nights
In which an aging brother's heart
Shrugs its shoulders
And begins the terrifying journey
To blossom.

Elegy
for Prince

Shout out to
Tough tender spirits
Alternately swaggering
And slow dancing
With silence.

Let the drummer take a cue
From the sound of high heels
On the earth.

A falsetto is sunlight
Set to music.

Longing was (and is)
My major —

But there are days
When you must create odes
To a magnificent booty

Taking your spirit
Around the world
In a day.

IV. Drafts

The following poems are transcribed from, and shown alongside scans of, Reuben's handwritten pages.

Home (Rain) 4/10/22
(draft)

God is my favorite drummer
she says to the dog
who never responds because
what to a dog does that mean
anymore than the month or day

Or the way she smiles
when the hyperactive weatherman
Calls for torrential showers /
Including her county
where the ratio of strip malls to solace
is as lopsided as the pillow they share

She kisses her couch mate
when the storm begins,
and quietly worries about Walter
who recently returned ~~with~~ from
3 months ~~with~~ family –
only to continue moving from
porch to porch
       like a ~~weathered~~ weathered
Chess piece –
       ~~Beca~~ Because, he
       proclaims, this is home

Home (Rain)

4/10/22
(draft)

God is my favorite drummer
she says to the dog
who never responds because
what to a dog does that mean
any more than the month or day

Or the way she smiles
when the hyperactive weatherman
Calls for torrential showers
Including her country
where the ratio of strip malls to solace
is as lopsided as the pillow they share

She kisses her couch mate
when the storm begins,
and quietly worries about Walter
who recently returned from
3 months with family—
only to continue moving from
porch to porch
like a weathered
chess piece—
Because, he
proclaims, this is home

Playing ~~The~~ ~~French~~ Horn

Our first date —
the four measure intro
~~to Sam Cooke's "Cupid"~~
Countermelody in
the key of longing

(Did the horns
really come from France?)

(~~What I mean is~~)
did I have to travel
in order to meet the sound?

How serendipitous
Mr. Capehart told me

The Orchestra was in   awkward
need of an ~~7th Grade~~
dreamer)

Before nodding
toward the scuffed
~~brown~~ case
brown

4/13/22
(draft)

Playing the French Horn

Our first date—
the four measure intro
to Sam Cooke's "Cupid"

Countermelody in
the key of longing

Did the horns
really come from France?

What I mean is
did I have to travel
in order to meet the sound?

How serendipitous
Mr. Capehart told me

The Orchestra was in
need of an awkward 7th grade
dreamer

Before nodding
toward the scuffed
brown case.

4/13/22
(draft)

Kelly Writers

~~Sad~~ Strange
~~and~~ and sad
~~strange~~ (~~reverse~~?)
how
we
cling
to
lands
our ~~aging~~ aging
hearts
no longer
recognize
5/7/22

(draft)

Kelly Writes

Strange
and sad
how
we
cling
to
lands
our aging
hearts
no longer
recognize

5/7/22
(draft)

Visiting The Fam
(on Mother's Day)

for Father
silence is
the way
he lived
(most of his
life) ? –

minus the daily
razor
and change of
well- pressed
clothing .

Nearby trees
nod like my
brother/
As I share
my (60 something ?) life –
No one offers wisdom

Or seems slighted
over the size. of
the overpriced
bouquet
hugging Mother's
stone .

5/8/22

Visiting the Fam
(on Mother's Day)

For father
silence is
the way he lived—
minus the daily
razor
and change of
well-pressed
clothing.

Nearby trees
nod like my
brother—
As I share
my (60 something?) life—
busy imbalanced life
like a finger painting
done in grade school

No one offers wisdom

Or seems slighted
over the size of
the overpriced
bouquet
hugging Mother's
stone.

5/18/22
(draft)

Riffy On The Inevitable #66
(*Jorry* The Ancestors)

when friends
use this term —
my first   (thought/question ?)
is
which
    ancestors (which ones?)
    ~~They (actually)~~ envision
    noble predecessors'
    who
        strode
        through this
        life / heads and
        culture held
                high /

        while I
        fear an eternity
        with kinfolk
        askin
        " when are you
            going back to chu "?

44

Kelly on the Inevitable #66
(Jesus the Ancestors)

When friends
use this term
my first
(thought/question?)
is
which
ancestors (which one?)
They envision
noble predecessors
who
strode
through this
life
heads and
culture held
high
While I
fear an eternity
with kinfolk
askin
"When are you
going back to church?"

(Kelly On The Inevitable #93)
(What Happens When You Die?)

I am (I'm)
     partial to
stories / in which
   the briefly
          deceased
          found/ ~~themselves~~
          in a restful,
          sunlit valley. I
                    be lieve
     The ~~truth I have~~
          in God,
               but would
                    prefer
          an eternity
               ~~minus~~ without
          authority
               figures

rocking
   pitch forks
     or
   ~~wings~~ wings
    unless the
     latter are
      slathered in
     ("genuine")
       pre-gentrification
       (gentrified)

      mumbo
       sauce.

(Kelly on the Inevitable #93)
(What Happens When You Die?)

I am (I'm)
partial to
stories
in which
the briefly
deceased
found
themselves
in a restful,
sunlit valley
I believe
in God,
but would
prefer
an eternity
without
authority
figures
rocking
pitchforks
or
wings
unless the
latter are
slathered in
(genuine)
pre-gentrification
(gentrified)
mumbo
sauce.

God bless those
who cared
for a brother
w more flaws
than a factory
second

God bless those

who cared
for a brother
with more flaws
than a factory
second

About the Author

Reuben Jackson (1956-2024) was a poet, jazz scholar, radio DJ, music critic, and Vermonter at heart born in Georgia and raised in Washington, DC. He graduated from Goddard College in 1978. After several years in DC, Jackson returned to Vermont and worked as an English teacher at Burlington High School and was a mentor with the Young Writers Project (www.youngwritersproject. org). He later hosted Friday Night Jazz on Vermont Public Radio from 2012 to 2018. Jackson served as the curator of the Smithsonian's Duke Ellington Collection in Washington, DC, and was the archivist with The University of The District of Columbia's Felix E. Grant Jazz Archives. His music reviews have been published in the *Washington Post, Washington City Paper, Jazz Times*, and featured on All Things Considered.

His poems have been published in over forty anthologies, including *This Is the Honey: An Anthology of Contemporary Black Poets*, edited by Kwame Alexander and published by Little, Brown and Company in 2024. His first volume of poetry, *fingering the keys*, which Joseph Brodsky picked for the Columbia Book Award, was published in 1991. His second collection, *Scattered Clouds: New & Selected Poems*, was published by Alan Squire Publishing in 2019. *My Specific Awe and Wonder* is his third book.

Acknowledgments

These poems, some in slightly different forms, were previously published:

"Dear Montpelier" in Voicing Art, a PoemCity edition of 'Love Poems to Montpelier' inspired by the photography of Cassandra M. Maniero, April 2021.

"Kelly Donaldson's Blues in ¾ Time," "Kelly Makes It Plain" and "Kelly Recalls 1963" in *Boston Review*, January 10, 2020.

"Key West" in *Scattered Clouds* (Alan Squire Publishing, 2019).

"Long Distance Love" in *PoemCity Anthology 2024* and PoemCity Montpelier (Kellogg-Hubbard Library, April 2024).

Publisher's Note

This book was completed after Reuben's untimely death (February 16, 2024), though it was a work in progress since he signed with Rootstock in November 2023. Reuben was thrilled to sign with a Vermont publisher for these "poems and whatnot," as he referred to them, and which he also called "a love letter to Vermont...with all the potholes visible." In one of our email exchanges, Reuben wrote: "I am very excited by all of this, and scared as shit...(Ah the writing life...LOL)." His inner critic was ever-present, and I did my best to reassure him that his poems are worthy, his genius palpable, and his words <u>matter</u>. I am ever grateful Reuben trusted me to publish this work, and also grateful to Jenae Michelle for her blessing and help in sending Reuben's handwritten drafts of poems from his desk for the posthumous "Drafts" section. The words and poems in the "Postscript" section were transcribed from a voicemail he sent on December 5, 2023. His voice is forever captured here, in the cloud, and in my heart.

Proceeds from the sale of this work will benefit a scholarship in his name at the University of the District Columbia for students interested in poetry and/or jazz.

Thank you to those who shared words of praise and words in tribute for this book: Abdul Ali, LN Bethea, Rajnii Eddins, Major Jackson, and Christopher Kaufman Illstrup.

Thank you to Rick Agran for guidance and encouragement, and to Michelle Singer for sending past PoemCity poems.

A special thanks to graphic designer and book formatter Eddie Vincent, who helped produce this book with integrity, keeping Reuben's wishes and aesthetic in mind.

And to all poets, speakers, and musicians who keep his spirit alive in performance and remembrance, a hearty thanks.

Reuben thrived in the community of love that surrounded him in both Washington, DC and Vermont. We miss him dearly. Thank you, dear reader, for engaging with Reuben's words. We hope you will pass on his message of love, beauty, and justice. I know wherever Reuben is (amongst the scattered clouds, perhaps), he is blushing while Black, and reaching for Kleenex.

Samantha Kolber, MFA
Publisher, Rootstock Publishing

Postscript: Voicemail from Reuben on December 5, 2023

Hey friends, how are you? It's Tuesday around 12:30 p.m. and I may or may not send this, but I'm going to record it, and, you know, let my soul be the guide or something like that. This is a draft of something I'm working on. I'm here at lunch and scribbling at lunch, maybe I'm trying to be like the poet Frank O'Hare doing those immortal lunch poems, albeit not as good, uh, but I have been thinking about, talking about, and I guess further processing parts of my life which have to do with or had to do with—well, code switching implies something else—but finding ways to get where you want to be at any given time. If, in the case of the piece I'm gonna share, your parents were very strict and, if the speaker, as they say in grad school, expressed too much exuberance, they probably would have kiboshed it. Anyway, that's kind of the impetus for this draft, it's tentatively titled:

How to Get There, 11th Grade Mix

Tell your parents
it's just some goofy weekend church retreat
somewhere beyond the city
and that the youth minister assigned you to lead
a creative writing session.

These lines must be uttered in the tone
which completely but temporarily gags
the desire to travel to the mountains and
Billy DeMarco's ancient hearse
on roads where your eyes will smile at every star.

Remember there is no such thing as overplaying
the "preacher made me do it" riff.
Your ultra pious folks equate his every breath
as dictation from God.

They like him
as much as they like your newfound solemnity
even though he's not Baptist.

Lower your head as if you were there
when they crucified their lord
then thanked Him and practiced
earnest tones.

Go to your room slowly,
pack your bag in the twilight
so that no one
no one
will see you smile.

Thanks for listening. Keep on keeping on, okay?
These are trying times. Trying AF. Bye-bye.

9 781578 691784